BEYOND THE BREAKERS

Discovering Your Best Life Beyond Circumstance

James Burgess

FOREWORD

Beyond the Breakers is an intriguing examination of the factors that lead to success in business leadership. As I read James' book, I sensed he was dealing more with success in life than just business. In fact, part of his treatise is that to be successful in business leadership, you have to be successful in life. I couldn't agree more. I found myself thoroughly enjoying the book as I read it. You will too!

As a psychologist for 36 years, I spend a lot of my time examining the root causes of the symptoms that motivate people to come for counselling. I was delighted to see that James also addresses the issue of root causes in his Everyday Compass. So much of modern day psychology and psychiatry focuses on treatment before the root of the problem has been examined and worked through. James' book is refreshingly bold in pointing to a better compass direction than much of what I have seen and read in present day psychology.

The "Everyday Compass" is a masterful tool to focus people on a vision for the future by examining what they believe, who they are connected with, where they have come from and where they are going. It enables people to see the direction they are facing in their present circumstances and what they can do for themselves to engage the journey of life successfully. I also appreciated that James' own faith journey has been a large part of finding meaningful direction for his life.

I loved how personal and honest James is in sharing his own story. Along with sharing the stories of other people, he has woven his own accounts of struggle and development so you can see that he is presenting principles of life that really work. James has been gifted with "the mandate of encouragement". I believe he has succeeded in this. Reading this book will aid you "to sail beyond your breakers".

Graham Bretherick
Registered Psychologist
President - Run Free Ministries

ACKNOWLEDGMENTS

To my wife Sharon,
my faithful companion
who is always on deck
no matter the weather!

For the Everyday Community,
clients, friends and fellow explorers

INTRODUCTION

Do we understand the value of time? How about the value of personal contribution? Or the value of progress and satisfaction inside a busy life? At what point do we finally take action to gain control, move past the past, and press onward to our preferred future?

For more than 18 years I have coached many diverse people in business and personal contexts. They all strived for a sense of identity, meaningful contribution, and direction.

Direction (in both business planning and personal growth) may be our plan for the near future but it builds upon our foundation of belief and action. Regardless of where we set our sights, our actions and principles will inevitably align and move us toward that destination so long as we choose to push forward.

However, the desire to achieve, build, or change something is necessary before the compass concept (which you will discover as you read on) can truly help us. As we progress through our lives, we need to develop a desire to become more in some fashion — rather than just sit back and coast through life and circumstance.

My company, Everyday Communities, was founded on the principles of direction and progression. It is less about aiming for a vague destiny and more about establishing destination and positive progress for life and business. We practice a true "progress vs. perfection" philosophy for coaching our client-member community.

We only have so much time and energy given to us in this world. How will we use it? What choices do we need to make to believe and act in ways that have influence and meaning in the world around us?

This book is about the journey of breaking free. It is about the discovery of personal authority and purpose. It is about mastering the lifetime art of exploration. This book has been lovingly crafted — and in some ways forged — to bring others into a greater sense of direction and impact while they still truly live.

PREPARING TO SET SAIL

"Whosoever wishes to know about the world must learn about it in its particular details. Knowledge is not intelligence.

In searching for the truth be ready for the unexpected. Change alone is unchanging.

The same road goes both up and down. The beginning of a circle is also its end. Not I, but the world says it: all is one.

And yet everything comes in season."

—*Heraklietos of Ephesos*

AN AIMLESS JOURNEY
Our Big Problem

"We can easily forgive a child who is afraid of the dark;
the real tragedy of life is when men are afraid of the light."
—*Plato*

The concept of floating aimlessly is scary. So many of us float with no anchor to what we believe, gathering undirected associations and carrying unnecessary baggage.

Not all of us are meant to be high-performing achievers; that would put our world in a constant state of panic! And many people are happy with their steady, cruise-control lifestyle which allows them to offer stability to those around them. I am not challenging that.

My big challenge — to everyone — is that when there is a choice, you need to be empowered to make it. Where there is a direction, to be motivated to take it. When there is opportunity to be restored, to be authentic and not to fake it. Simply, to move and not to be stagnant.

I suggest rewatching the Tom Hanks' movie Castaway with this is mind. You will quickly see the parallels of being caught in a life where time rushed by when suddenly your path, purpose, and schedule was taken from you. Something in your life or business went sideways and you found yourself shipwrecked and directionless, so-to-speak. How do you recover?

What you thought was going to be your life is now delayed or even rendered unreachable. You had a plan, a great plan. You took the courses, got your degrees, and somehow you discover you float in places you never expected or asked to be.

You look around and discover the people you spend time with move at the same slow pace of progression and achievement as you. Right now, you recall the feeling that you could somehow rise to another level and achieve something more valuable in the world. That feeling is speaking to you from the inside. You long for a higher quality of life and experience. Now what?

FLOATING

Will sat at his desk, in the middle of a busy week, preparing for his next meeting.

Themes in his coaching practice seemed to come in seasons and this week was all about "keeping the boat steady" for his clients and finding new ways for them to achieve success in their small businesses.

The phone rang. A man on the other line spoke up, "My name is John. We met some time ago at a business-to-business function."

"John!" Will responded. "Great to hear from you. How can I help you today?"

John paused, then continued, hesitantly, "I was wondering if you would be available to meet with me over lunch this week?"

Will looked over his calendar and quickly responded, "Yeah, does Thursday work for you?"

"That would be great," John replied. "I appreciate it."

"Is there anything specific I should prepare for?"

Another brief pause. "Not really," John said, finally. "I would just like to continue our conversation from before. I have some thoughts on what you were presenting to me that evening." Will made a note and booked the date into his calendar.

"No problem John, I would be happy to connect over lunch."

"I'll see you Thursday," John responded. "Thanks, Will. Much appreciated!"

Thursday afternoon turned out bright and warm. The two men greeted each other warmly and sat down on the café patio to escape the mid-day hustle and bustle of the staff and patrons.

As the waiter took their order, Will conducted a quick study of the many people all around, discussing business ideas or sharing personal stories. Thinking of all the interesting stories being shared always fascinated him. People's lives were like an unfolding map, an adventure to discover.

Not long after their meals were delivered, John shifted the conversation from friendly chat to a more intense description of his personal life and how he felt about it. Will — who had been coaching for over 12 years at the time — knew right away that John had a burden to unload and listened with great interest. Over the next hour John let it all out, his bearing heavy with stress, pressure, unmet expectations, and weariness.

John shared his professional and personal struggles, from battling boredom and failing to find meaning in his career, his troubled marriage, getting his son through the rigours of amateur sports in the hopes of going pro, and the pains of his relationship with his troubled teenage daughter. Will could not help but feel a great compassion for his new friend.

Despite his passion for helping people crying out to be put to use, what could he offer someone who has had years to accumulate fear, frustration, and dissatisfaction? He knew this could not be fixed in a day and certainly not over lunch!

There was no question; John was lost. Like so many Will had worked with before, he felt this man was worth so much as an individual but that value was buried under the pressures of a fast-paced career and, as he described, an unrewarding personal life.

Finally, John transitioned the conversation back to Will and asked a simple question, "As a coach, what do you think?"

It was a big question that expected a weighty answer. Sometimes Will did not feel prepared for this kind of responsibility when people expressed a lifetime of struggle so openly. However, John was here in a moment of vulnerability, and Will felt hopeful.

John was not beyond help; but what kind of help? In all his years of coaching, Will learned that coaching serves the larger population who say, "I am not sick enough to need therapy, but I know I need something more in my life." He concluded that his new friend was just such a person.

After some thought, Will felt he had an accurate take on the situation and responded, "After all you've said, I see a man in a small boat in the middle of the ocean. This man is leaning over the side, peering into the deep looking for the compass he lost along the way. John, you are a good man, and we need to find your compass." That was all.

John looked at Will with astonishment. Was his answer just that simple?

Not so. Will continued, "The big picture doesn't reveal all the details. It's only when we take on the journey of healthy self-examination and begin taking steps for improvement that we will uncover those details. You know, all those dreams, passions, and purposes of our life that seem to get shoved away into the background drowned by the busy-ness and aimless associations that take up our time and talent."

John realized he was floating. Will helped him to understand that this was brought on by his family situation was to blame, but that John, himself, had not taken the time to define a preferred future. Even if it did not take exact shape, he would still progress with positive momentum; building prosperity and hope for himself and his family.

By the end of their time together, Will was happy to provide perspective and John felt hope again. There was still a long way to go to navigate through to that preferred future. Both men acknowledged that fact, but their time ended with mutual respect and positive perspectives.

>*"He who is enslaved by the compass has the freedom of the seas."*
>
>*—Unknown*

WITHOUT DIRECTION

Kylee was a smart, successful small-business woman. She had extensive experience in media and marketing and her ability to build communication with people was outstanding. She had a way, both focused and deliberate, of creating warm dialogue in an everyday kind of manner while maintaining her professionalism.

Around the time Will met Kylee, he was setting up a workshop focusing on personal growth for professional results. He was working on new concepts and the workshop was a work-in-progress. The knowledge and experience were top notch and applicable, but more was being added.

At a business-to-business group meeting, Kylee expressed great interest in this workshop. Will's initial thought was "Why? This person seems to have it all together!" Regardless, Will invited Kylee to participate in the workshop.

The workshop had a small group of a dozen or so participants, from all types of industries, and Will was excited by their sense of discovery.

As the workshop progressed, the participants were all keen to contribute — a good sign for Will. Kylee was no exception; she had a lot to say and all of it was good! Her experiences in her past media career were invaluable.

At a particular point of the workshop, the group was set to complete an exercise in communication. Will saw it as one of the most challenging segments of the workshop. The group was tasked to pull information from the presenter by asking questions in a specific style. As they got closer to describing the presenter's mind-picture, the participants were rewarded with more information on the white board. The idea was to challenge the group's ability to gather the right information without resorting to default tactics like yes or no answers.

As the exercise progressed, the tension mounted and frustration set in. Certain participants persevered, while others were resigned to failure, and still others displayed signs of outright anger that their

11

questions were not netting the information that they expected: Will always looked forward to the debriefing of this particular excercise.

Kylee, however, showed signs of emotion. This was a different — unexpected— reaction from the other participants. She was beginning to crack under some invisible pressure. Will realized he needed to pause the exercise to provide perspective and Kylee excused herself for a few minutes.

Upon her return, Will interrupted the discussion to ask gently how she was. Kylee responded honestly.

"I am feeling a strong pressure to perform and I feel the sense of failure that has been in my life since I was a child."

She felt vulnerable enough to describe what she felt this feeling was based upon and shared her inner conflict of confidence and performance.

The group listened with respect. Will knew that people were either thinking, "That is so me; I am taking notes!" or "Man, I am glad that is not me; but I better take note!" Rarely would they disrespect a moment like that — if they did, they were silent anyway.

The air was thick with the realities that Kylee presented. Everyone connected on an intimate level and Will could see that something was at work in the group as a whole. It was one of the most profound experiences he had seen in a workshop in all his time facilitating. The group needed it.

After this experience, Kylee and Will worked together on her business and often conversed about her feelings and attitude about that day. Will kept an encouraging attitude toward Kylee's story. He knew that coaching was not always about hardcore progress. Sometimes it was a quiet ear to allow his clients to breathe and get it out. He knew from experience that the need to be heard is just as important as the need to be healed.

In one particular conversation Kylee expressed her frustration about achieving a sense of destination and a life of significance.

"Sometimes, Will," she said. "I have to shout it out: when will it be my turn! It feels like I am spinning my wheels, trying to gain some kind of acceptance from people and no matter how hard I work at it, it's never enough. Another hoop, another test. When is it my turn?"

Kylee had all the signs of success, but inside she was cracking. Will took notes and took time to contemplate these conversations. His conclusion focused on direction. Kylee showed signs of not having a firm set of beliefs and values surrounding her life and talents. She was stuck in the "hamster wheel" of performance, trying to meet the satisfactions of others — and there was always more had to be done, said, or given.

To find personal significance, Kylee needed to set her own direction, recognize her particular contributions and how they gave positive impact, and establish new and encouraging relationships. She had to grab the compass and set a new course!

> *"God gave us the gift of life; it is up to us to give ourselves the gift of living well."*
>
> —*Voltaire*

WE ALL NEED...

Over his years of coaching, Will journaled his experiences not just to keep track or cover off issues for liability, but also to keep mindful of the grand adventure. Writing down these experiences widened his perspectives, created useful curiosities, and allowed for powerful innovations in his work. One such story was Dave.

Dave was a young competitive body builder, who could perform great feats of strength. He was into competitive contact sports and loved to talk about them all day long! Dave was good-natured and kind to people.

When Will first met Dave he was impressed with this young man and what he desired to do in his life.

Dave loved working with youth. It was his passion. He desired to give them a sense of self worth and direction founded upon his Christian principles. Dave wanted so much to provide a safe haven for young people: he felt this was his life's calling. Will and Dave often met for coffee to discuss Dave's direction.

Dave was well known in his circles to be supportive and loved to help when he believed enough in a cause. This is where things began to take a less than savoury turn for Dave. Over the years of their relationship, Will noticed some significant things about Dave and how he related to people.

Dave got involved in a large fundraising project to build a club in his community for young people. By all indications he was to become a lead coach in the club itself and lent his knowledge of fitness and leadership to the project. Dave threw himself into the project with everything he had.

The project became more significant with funds raised and a location chosen, and Dave was invited to move into the unfinished facility. He was so happy. Will and Dave spoke often of the vision for this club and what it would be like as things came together. Dave really took personal ownership over this project and it showed.

After about 6 months of working with the planning committee and other more prominent public figures, Dave started to notice that communication drifted off. He noticed that he was not brought into the meetings or consulted as much as he was in the beginning. Dave soon discovered that those in the driver's seat of the initiative had other plans for the maturing project and that Dave's involvement and contributions were becoming less relevant. Dave was crushed. He had been moved out of the centre of the action and began to despair.

Dave retreated from his involvement in the project. He became less involved and less passionate. When he and Will met, Dave focused on how he was betrayed and questioned everything he believed about people.

During one particular conversation, Will felt he had heard enough of Dave's heart and hurt to delve deeper.

He asked, "Dave, what was your upbringing like?"

Dave thought for a few seconds and then went into a long description of his family and relationships with them. Will listened patiently.

Dave described that his parents divorced when he and his older brother were young and their parents were at war throughout their upbringing. Dave stated that his brother was his dad's favourite. He described how his brother would often receive support for his endeavours where Dave himself would get a more indifferent kind of treatment from his dad.

Their mom had moved away and they had less opportunity to visit her. Dave made several attempts to solicit help from his mom over the years but inside he really wanted his dad's approval. He was jealous of his brother and wanted to be given the same favour from his dad. Sadly, by the way Dave described it all, that favour was not given. That fact did not stop Dave from trying.

It was apparent that Dave was interested in seeking approval and belonging. He shared his numerous disappointments in his life with Will and his inability to truly belong anywhere even though he looked like he did. Will saw that Dave was quick to wear his heart on his sleeve, giving a full effort at every opportunity.

However, Will realized that Dave's reasons for this effort were not entirely authentic, in that Dave was suffering inside from the rejection he felt from his family life.

Over the next few months, Dave retreated and contact became less and less between Dave and Will. After a few attempts to reach out, Will knew he had to release Dave to his own journey.

Over the next few years Dave showed up out of the blue with different projects he was getting involved with. Will knew that Dave was searching. As they shared lunch one day, Will decided to challenge Dave.

"Dave, why not settle into a community and begin to build some stability for yourself?"

Dave floundered a bit before he could get a real answer out. So many reasons and justifications describing why that would not be possible. He was taken off guard.

Will ventured another challenge, "I have known you for a while. I believe you have a desire to really contribute and that you truly have a lot to give. It seems that you deeply want to be accepted and be engaged in a purpose-filled cause, but it will take work. It will take a fundamental change in how you see people and how you overcome your very non-committal behavior."

During the course of this conversation Dave began to see how his experiences had created bad habits and bad interpretations of others. He knew he wanted to be wanted. He knew he needed to be needed. He also knew that he loved the thought of being really cared for. Will affirmed that his desire to belong somewhere was not a weakness but a strong natural desire that we all have.

Dave needed community. Dave desired purpose!

> *"The purpose of life seems to be to acquaint a man with himself and whatever science or art or course of action he engages in reacts upon and illuminates the recesses of his own mind. Thus friends seem to be only mirrors to draw out and explain to us ourselves; and that which draws us nearer our fellow man, is, that the deep Heart in one, answers the deep Heart in another, — that we find we have (a common Nature) — one life which runs through all individuals, and which is indeed Divine."*
> —Ralph Waldo Emerson

THE COMPASS

The compass to the Everyday Community is really quite simple but it took time to come to this destination. It is based on the assumption that:

Direction displaces despair &
Destination sharpens the resolve to fulfill destiny.

It also provides a four-point reference for progress. The compass for our client-community affirms the greater value of their progress as opposed to the value of being perfect. We will take more time to define this better later on in the book.

Over the last 18 years, I have had the greatest pleasure to serve so many. It has been an adventure in assisting them each to find their way and figure out the problems plaguing their small business models. Overall, I provided practical, tactical, and simple inspirational support.

I first started out in the late 90's as an independent professional sales trainer. It started by asking a big, "What if" question. It was a question that recognized a problem and demanded that I work on a solution.

One day I looked around in my place of employment and thought to myself, "What if we had a sales training course that was character-based instead of a straight system-based model?" It was the seed of what was to become Everyday Communities, a coaching company dedicated to everyday entrepreneurs and everyday people!

It took these 18 years for us to evolve into a great community-based coaching model with all of the services a small-business team would need! But this was not without some pain. I can tell you that my wife Sharon and I have had our own journey to sail and what we learned from it has been invaluable not only to our own family but to the many others we decided to share it with. We walked what we talk. This is where the best foundations are established when you consider engaging a coaching professional.

Throughout the years, I recognized through my business mentoring and coaching experiences that the corporate environments that I was working with needed a positive influence within.

As a business coach, I often helped individuals but noticed that they needed more than just a one-day workshop to realize the success they desired over the long term.

That was the beginning of the inspiration for creating the Everyday Communities.

The Result

Everyday Communities is a name chosen because success and growth does not happen in a one-day or one-week seminar, but rather on an everyday basis within a community that contains like-minded people looking to achieve similar results and share common interests.

A healthy community can often provide the shared experience and build effective process together with a little guidance. This foundational understanding literally jumped out at me one day, while I casually scanned the bookshelf at my local bookstore.

INSPIRATION STRIKES

I found myself stuck in the rut of chasing the next opportunity — leeching my command over my craft every time I asked permission to offer service or was evaluated unfairly for my unorthodox approach to coaching.

Rewind to late 2009. I had the honour of mentoring a young guy named Charles.

Charles had come into my office one day for an interview for a sales position we had advertised for my friend's small promotions company. My role was to provide business development consulting and to design the sales process for this company. This included interviewing and approving candidates for hire.

Charles sat down in his casual shirt, full beard, and round rimmed glasses and politely thanked me for meeting with him. I started with why he felt that a sales opportunity was for him. He responded, "Because I know that if I learn sales, I will never be without work." This answer was enough for me. After a few more questions and conversation Charles was hired, not because of his competency, but because of his attitude. I saw something in this young guy that I felt needed to be nurtured.

The next three months were all about teaching the "nuts and bolts" of selling. Promotional product sales is not an easy industry to get your feet wet in, but it was what Charles had chosen. Every day I came into the office to see him grinding away at cold-calls and persevering through rejection after rejection. The guy was determined, and my respect for him grew.

I taught him that cold-calling is the best therapy to overcome the feeling of being rejected. It is not personal. If he mastered this part of the journey, he could withstand the pain of other vital areas of his training.

We finally got to the stage where I needed to introduce him to networking. Networking is the process of building contacts and advocates in business who would refer or champion your business over time. It is a vital process that can assist in stabilizing cash flow for any small business. Charles was eager to take it up a notch!

Monday morning arrived and I took him out for coffee. I remember telling him some of my own past networking adventures of — some funny and others painful.

I concluded with a challenge. "Do you think you can rally twelve of your best contacts and sit down with them to discuss your endeavour?"

Charles quickly and confidently responded, "Yes."

I sent him out to accomplish this challenge. I felt it necessary for him to make his own discoveries here. He needed to learn the pain of having an unclear vision. He needed to hear the objections of people he respected and figure out how he would convince them to support his work. After waiting two weeks, I checked in with him.

"How goes the challenge?" I asked.

"Not so good," he responded.

We sat down again and reviewed his action steps and the walls he kept hitting with people he thought were his best chance to build a referral network. As he described his journey, I was reminded of my own process.

Networking was not just about having the ability to rally people to a cause, it was also about keeping the ego in check with the realization that just because we think something is important, it does not mean that others will see it with the same sense of importance.

Calmly and encouragingly I told Charles, "Some things need to be caught, not taught, and there is no course you can take that will guarantee people's loyalty to you."

He understood exactly what I was saying: people are not lab rats, nor tools to be used. They are valuable assets. All businesses need to remember that. Without the love and loyalty of the people, there is no business.

I asked Charles to allow me to show him how to create something remarkable instead of just looking for the next sale. He gave me his permission to show him and his support once we got it moving.

Around this time, another friend and I were discussing the trials of small business ownership and I shared with him what I was doing with Charles. He said, "It sounds like you work with the everyday entrepreneur. You know, those who start from the ground up. The ones who make up the majority of the marketplace." This description sat well with me.

Charles and I planned the structure for this new business-to-business group. We drafted mission and value statements and fleshed out a vision for this group we intended to put into motion.

When it came to figuring out what this thing would be called, it was easy. "Let's take the pressure off," I said. "Let's call this the Everyday Entrepreneur Community of Business."

Charles was enthusiastic with this. He was excited to get started and in his excitement he asked, "Okay, we got this. Now what?"

Laughing together, we set to work in sending out direct invitations to my contact network to come and join us for a special vision casting of this new group. We targeted twenty-two good people and contacted them directly, before sending them all the information for the event. Everything needed to be organized and thought out. Our message had to be clear.

Our big evening came two weeks later. We were nervous about the final attendance. I have learned over the years that even though people tell you they will participate in something, it does not count for much until they actually show up. That night sixteen of the twenty-two invited showed up!

We described the overall vision, the concept, and the features going forward. There were enthusiastic responses all the way through.

The critical moment came. Looking over the small audience I asked, "We are looking to establish this new group right away. Tonight I ask you, are you in or are you out?" Of course I was polite and diplomatic here but the question was simple and direct and required a simple and direct response. The response came and we were shocked. Fifteen out of the sixteen in attendance were ready to sign up that night.

Now we had a purpose. A mandate was given for us to develop our member-community and provide them with a superior networking experience. Over the next few months we improved the meeting template and added more features for the membership. The community began to grow. Even though Charles moved away eight months later, the Community took flight!

POSITIVE DEVIANCE

From time-to-time I like to go to places like a bookstore or office supply store just to walk the aisles and look around. It inspires me. I can hone in on my own business development needs when I stroll. This particular stroll ended up becoming worth much more than a good idea.

As I scanned the shelf, I spotted a cool-looking book with a hand print on the spine. The title piqued my curiosity: "The Power of Positive Deviance" written by Richard Pascale, Jerry Sternin and Monique Sternin. It focused on how unlikely innovators solve the world's toughest problems. I was excited to pick this one up!

After scanning the pages and the author bios, I decided to take the chance and buy it. I took it home and began reading in earnest. At that time in my business history, I was hungry for knowledge. I wanted to explore new ideas on how to coach better.

Up until this point I had been chasing business, chasing opportunity, and finding the grind to be frustrating (I was in the same place as my competition, and I wanted to stand out).

The positive deviance concept is a way of honouring what is already present within people. Coaching this way elevates people and respects their life and talents before needing to directly coach them individually. This is not to say that there is no need for individual attention. It is to say that we can save our client-community tons of money and provide them with a wider source of inspiration. We are now better able to walk side-by-side with our client-members.

This concept of working with people this way really jazzed me. I thought about how I wanted to grow my coaching business and realized that this was the approach I needed to take.

I felt I had to build something that attracted people and provide them with tangible results. The greater vision was to open up the bridge of trust and engage them in other areas of need. It became all about discovery and relationship.

The community was growing and I needed to organize the services — a big task, since I was very busy working in the business and not so much on it. The positive deviance concept opened up my eyes to see a more natural way of engaging people with strength and calm authority. It took the pressure off. I did not have to chase it all anymore and that made me a happy coach!

As I read the book through, I affirmed that many points were already being employed within the Everyday Entrepreneur Community. I might be a positive deviant! As a coach, I had to develop these concepts further and apply them to our community experience. There was so much value hidden inside our membership. The challenge was to get the members to see it and act accordingly.

My direction was set and I could see it through to its fulfillment.

"Positive deviance (PD) is founded on the premise that at least one person in a community, working with the same resources as everyone else, has already licked the problem that confounds the others. This individual is an outlier in the statistical sense — an exception, someone who deviates in a positive way from the norm. In most cases this person does not know he or she is doing anything unusual."

—The Power of Positive Deviance: Pascale, Sternin, Sternin

SETTING SAIL

LEADERSHIP
How Do We Pilot This Thing?

The development of our methodology and philosophies for coaching was serpentine.

I would like to outline briefly some of the more pivotal evolutions we encountered along the way. The first was my own sense of leadership and the change in my style as a coach. This would later bring great value to the community, as well as to the clientele we served outside of the membership.

In 2003, I had the privilege of meeting someone whom I grew to respect as a mentor. He challenged me in ways I had never been challenged before. Daniel was decisive and focused, with successful endeavours on his record as well as significant failures to which he was not ashamed to admit. He was a strong and wise man that I knew I could receive from.

Daniel challenged me to figure out exactly what it was that I wanted out of this life. He required me to write down my life goals. These goals were more than paying off the house or raising great kids (though that is always a goal worthy of acknowledgement). He wanted to know what my desire for impact was, what my life calling was before I finished my race on this planet.

It was like I was smashed in the face by a boxer's right hook! It was easy for me to step up to this challenge because I was eager to learn and grow in my talents and personal wellbeing. I eventually wrote down six personal life goals and four main values in which I believed. These four values are what would later influence the formation of the Everyday Compass philosophy.

What I truly believed to be important in the pursuit of healthy life were **Life, Love, Liberty, and Progress**. What do these mean exactly?

Life
Discovering a fuller life experience and new things. Understanding what adds to me as a person and having the

knowledge of what takes quality of life away from me, is what helps me achieve a youthful and vibrant sense of wellbeing.

Love

Exploring and enjoying the relationships in my life, first to God, then to my family, and inevitably to the world around me. Knowing that without a greater sense of love, I am ineffective and stagnant in my pursuits. I believe God loves me and has created me in His image. I actively discover daily what that image is.

Liberty

Enjoying the heartbeat of freedom from things that seek to rob me of my purpose, potential, and ability. Knowing and living a release from the past and being empowered to reach into my preferred future.

Progress

Actively seeking to embrace change in my life. With forward thinking, I desire to walk with patience, and wisdom. I desire to have a bigger vision of the more important things in life. I will actively and continually take hold of an attitude of discovery and not one of continual recovery.

Lackluster Engagement

Once these goals and values were written, it became ever more clear to me that the direction my wife and I were headed was sound and that I was becoming better prepared to handle what would later become a very purposeful life.

Sharon and I have always walked together as a team. Through our years together, she had to grow in her own way alongside me. I respect her for all she has done and the stabilizing effect she has had on me through these years. Passion sometimes needs stability!

In early 2011, I was working diligently to meet with current member-clients as well as networking hard to meet new prospective members for the community. The financial model was functioning and the meeting schedule was consistent. People enjoyed this new style of networking and had a lot of praise for it. Still, I noticed the level of engagement was quite superficial.

Do not get me wrong, there were some in the community who were strong supporters, but for the rest it was looking like a repeat of everything else out there. I was frustrated by this. They were missing out on so much!

Feeling ready to kick something, I began to pace the floor in my home. Sometimes a good passionate pacing is all it takes to gain clarity. I am a praying man and I believe that answers come to those who are willing to listen. This was one of those situations.

Once calmed, I wrote in my journal. I described what was going on and what I needed to do about it. Clarity came as my pen scribbled! I realized four key issues that I was facing at the time. Allow me to share with you the first three keys in this parable that was written in those moments of clarity.

THE PARABLE OF THE FARMER

One day, a young businessman paced the floor of his living room thinking about a certain vision for building business and feeling a little agitated. He had been working at a few projects over the previous couple of years but with limited results to show for it.

In his frustration, he began to speak aloud as if lodging a complaint. As he spoke, his thoughts began to unscramble and certain aspects about building his dream business became more clear. Pondering what success could look like he realized that success in anything was a 3-stage process.

Stage 1: Sowing
(Invent, Invest)

The first stage was like a farmer in his field. In his mind's eye he pictured this farmer sowing seeds from his pack in a liberal fashion. The ground had been tilled and prepared properly; the conditions were right before the seeds were sown.

Realization #1

The young man realized that he needed to prepare before the actual investment was made into his dream business. Planning, making strong contacts, gathering resources and proper funding, and most of all establishing and sharing a clear and articulated vision.

Realization #2

In the vision, the young man saw seeds being sown and that the farmer knew that out of the multitudes of seed thrown into the ground that many might not germinate, some would germinate and grow with limited results, but many more would grow to produce a real harvest. Knowing the risk involved, the farmer continued to sow.

The young businessman realized at this moment that he had been "sowing" or investing his knowledge and efforts with a premature expectation of results. He realized he had not previously been willing to pay proper attention to his investments. They had been like the seed that produced only limited results.

Realization #3

Understanding the risk of his endeavours, he imagined the farmer weighing all the factors and making the decision to continue sowing all of the seeds he carried with the intention of gaining a higher potential of return.

The young man realized that investing is always a risk. He also realized that if all the preparation work was done properly, that he would gain to the level he had committed. He needed to invest heavily instead of sparingly. He needed to invest intelligently, not blindly. He knew he needed to commit to the success of the investment with more patience.

His First Conclusion

The need to invest time and resources properly is essential to building success. However, many of us have not been willing to make those real commitments required to build something remarkable. Instead, the vast majority of people consider a successful business effort like a micro-wave dinner: fast and easy. We want to harvest as soon as the seed hits the soil. Our impatience creates a stunted result and we lose out on what could have been if we had only committed a little more.

Stage 2: Cultivate
(Experiment, Innovate, Change, Discover, Refine)

The young man was not finished. He realized that investing his time and effort was not all that was required. Like starting an engine, it takes a lot of energy in the beginning to achieve the right amount of power for forward movement. Now the real work had begun!

After making all preparations and defining his business vision, he began connecting with his most valuable and loyal contacts in order to share his vision. He realized the task at hand was not to invest or "sow" but it was now to share the message and "cultivate" the field where he had made his investments of time, vision, and effort.

The young man realized that his efforts needed to take root in the minds of his contacts. As he shared, people began asking more questions to learn more, and as they did, he made time to meet with each one. This process went on for months.

Realization #1

Cultivating a vision takes intentional effort and consistent contact. It takes meaningful dialogue and passion. This is the time where any vigilant entrepreneur can pick up vital, objective feedback and create innovative solutions to certain gaps found in the original business idea.

Sometimes it is not predictable. To prepare for this unpredictability is to be open for essential feedback from which to enact positive change or innovation.

Remember, if this vision was just about how it makes you feel, all entrepreneurial efforts would be incredibly successful. The truth is this vision is about how it makes others feel and whether they will value it enough to pay for it.

Realization #2

As the young man proceeded to cultivate the vision, he began to formulate a greater understanding of his business idea and its perceived value in the eyes of his potential clientele. He was able to determine with more accuracy and less speculation a comprehensive service delivery and pricing strategy. In some circumstances, he absorbed a financial cost in trade for all of the valuable information he was receiving.

You may be asking: "What do I do to cultivate?"

- Know what you are offering. Define it. Understand its applications and who can use it.
- Take the risk and share your idea/service/product with people who have an obvious interest.
- Take the time to test out value by surveying. Ask them specifically what they might value this great idea/service/product in dollars and cents.
- Find the intestinal fortitude to ask for referrals. Who else would most benefit from what you offer?

- Innovate from the valuable feedback you receive. Be prepared for change and remember that the coming change could be the one key aspect for a multiplication of future results.
- Spread the message! Make your business easy and accessible to engage with. Be available!

His Second Conclusion

Testing, surveying, and cultivating relationships is an essential part of any small business development. When resources are limited it is only your two hands that can cultivate for results.

Stage 3: Harvest
(Communicate, Strategize, Reap, Measure, Enjoy, Level Up!)

By this time, the young businessman had followed through on all that his vision had revealed. He had committed to the process of refining his business concept. He had taken time to cultivate the business, cultivate relationships. He had achieved the vital task of creating a demand for what he offered.

Now was the time to begin realizing the reward, the harvest for all his toil. He assessed his business model and worked hard to minimize glitches and gaps so as to increase the value of the client experience. He needed only one last thing to achieve the next level: positioning.

In the businessman's vision, the farmer cultivated all he could, but he needed to give his fields time to grow. As he watched diligently over his field, providing the right nutrients and paying more attention to areas that needed more attention, the farmer now prepared his equipment to handle the incoming harvest.

Realization #1

Are we ready for the demand to come? Have we structured our internal processes to handle the flow of information and developed the tools needed for the client to enjoy what they were promised? Establishing the right structure for client information — processes for client progression through your services — is essential before the flood of demand begins.

If we are not ready (we have not prepared our equipment like the farmer has), we will most likely experience a lot of unnecessary frustration and client disillusionment.

Realization #2

The young businessman realized he would need to connect strategically with other businesses that work consistently with more people than he could at this time. Through the cultivation stage, he had built several positive business-to-business alliances where his service would provide his partnerships with added value and goodwill in the minds of their clients. With a small budget to advertise with, this strategy became vital to the survival of his fledgling business.

His Third Conclusion

Through this journey he had come to fully respect the process which gained him valuable wisdom. Wisdom for what? Wisdom to do it all over again but with better results.

Can You See the Bigger Picture?

Is it not great that you have achieved some success and now can produce a better repeat performance?

Yes, this was where I was. I was the young businessman. It was another one of those ah-ha moments where personal experience brought high value and clarity to this Everyday vision. Not a lot in this parable is rocket science. It certainly wasn't brand new knowledge, but it was packaged all together to open up a new understanding and patience for me to continue. For that I am thankful!

Fourth Key

The fourth key was something I needed so that I could grow this vision beyond the reach of my own two hands. Before I explain the fourth key, I have to say that up until this time, I was a very independent person. I had recovered from recent betrayals in outside business endeavours and had carried an attitude that nobody was going to do things for me.

So, in certain areas I was healthy and enthusiastic but in other, more hidden, areas I carried unresolved anger. This fourth key was profound and would prove to be my freedom as the Everyday vision became more mature.

I realized that as a coach or leader of people it was incredibly important that I get my ego in check. It was funny because there I was, building a community that was designed to bring people together to achieve success but hypocritically, I was acting as a complete independent. This was an attitude that I knew was not the true me but had become reality because of my prior experiences.

As I studied the coaching, consulting, and motivational industry, I saw that people constantly look for the new flavor of the month. The great audiences were consumer driven, always looking for the next motivational or get-rich-quick fix. This, I decided, was not what I wanted the Everyday vision to be. It had to be something more and something long lasting.

The fourth key was simple to me. Get out of the way.

As a coach, I know I do not have to have all the answers. I have often used the term "guru" to describe people in my industry, and there are many. There certainly nothing wrong with being a guru-type teacher but I felt it was a role that could only last a season in the lives of people.

Over time I have learned that truly hungry people need something in life that lasts longer than a season. They need something substantial that had the potential to be relevant for a lifetime!

To become a gardener was my conclusion. This is not a game of presenting the latest trendy tips, tricks, or tools for living. This Everyday thing had to be something bigger than that.

Now, I am not a good gardener in the traditional sense of the word. In fact, my front yard looks like the house on the block that the kids avoid on Halloween! But the concept of stewarding an environment of growth was not lost on me.

When I was a boy, I was really excited to plant a single orange seed in an empty fish bowl. After filling it with dirt, I placed the seed into the soil and placed the bowl on the window sill where it could catch the sunlight.

After a few days, a bright green leaf sprouted, breaking through the surface of the dirt. You can imagine my anticipation of those juicy oranges I would get to eat!

Several days passed and that single leaf grew into a long stalk poking out above the rim of the bowl. How exciting! Until I noticed a much larger, but singular leaf popping up from the dirt.

I was confused! Was that long, fast growing thing not my glorious orange tree? Nope, it was a weed. Upon this revelation, I lost my patience and discarded the whole project. My disappointment dictated my premature abandonment of the project.

As my college professor once said when discussing leadership, "Sometimes, slow growth is good growth. The roots grow deep and long lasting when we have the patience to cultivate."

A gardener is diligent in creating the right conditions for growth to happen. The right treatment of the soil, water, fertilizer, and exposure to sunlight is what it takes for the garden to grow.

So, why can we not put this concept to work for our Everyday community?

As a leader of this vision, I determined to create something always honouring the life and business experiences of those involved, then provide a structure that assisted in the nurturing of communication which then provides opportunity for shared experiences (positive deviance behavior). This is where our community, those who truly got what we were all about, prospered and in more ways than one.

I do not want you to think that we only focus on people in business. However, they do seem to have more of a clear handle on the value of personal coaching and consulting as it relates to their life in business. These principles work well in family coaching and general life coaching, but for the sake of my story, it just happens to have a stronger pull toward the entrepreneurs.

The transition from my attitude and approach of "guru" to gardener was easy for me and crucial to the future success of the Everyday vision. Coaching people is a long-term experience. It is a journey of patience and perseverance. The idea of racing to have the best, the biggest, or the latest trendy methods or systems of success training is not that appealing to me anymore.

I know that there will always be others out there ready to start their "universities of success," but I love the everyday entrepreneur, the everyday people that are the salt of the earth. As a coach, I believe long-term relationships are what will sustain a community and bring prosperity to it as the world gets ever more challenging to thrive in.

WHEN THE STUDENT IS READY...

In the opening section, I gave three major examples of people who, on the surface, had their lives together. A closer examination revealed a darker side; a side a little more shadowed, that needed to be covered. These are aspects that fear the light of exposure, possible humiliation, or being assessed and found wanting.

Our fears about how others will perceive our weaknesses or imperfections are ever-present, no matter what books we read or courses we take. The battle for significance and value resides in us all.

Everyone has a journey, a timeline to be traveled. No matter our experiences, we still travel it, whether we like it or not.

You might be thinking, "Yes, but there are days I just want to hop off or resign from this timeline and blend back into obscurity!"

To that I would say, "Perhaps, but the timeline still moves forward; your speed of progression has just slowed for a time." Either way, it still proceeds.

We cannot always control the experiences we face, but we can choose how we receive them, understand them, and utilize the lessons learned. So many wander without mentorship in life. When you think of all the broken families in our society, you can imagine so many children having to find their way and personal identity by painful process of elimination. They were given no compass to help them through.

I feel that the concept of coaching and mentoring is so strong in our present time because of weak family and community bonds. All over our society we can see the results of abandonment, anger, and resentment that yearn for those missing moral and relational pillars that make people great. Regardless of where we are as individuals, we still desire to be mentored.

What that looks like for each person varies depending on all kinds of factors.

My own quest for mentoring is no different. I grew up in a single-parent home. My mother worked and attended post-secondary

37

school to achieve her degree in chemical technology. She was a hard worker who diligently pursued her goals. That was her journey.

While her story progressed, my own did as well. A tough school experience, angry and not knowing why, and always getting into fights with teachers and fellow students alike. I liked to be involved in activities but found myself gravitating toward solo sports.

One junior high experience was participating in long-distance running. I had a coach who spoke plainly and did not waste time on trivial things. He was firm and fair. We were a group of runners, but he worked with us first as individuals, then as a team. We made it to the regional finals that year.

All through the season we practiced. Running kilometres as a team. The fastest kid was Kenny. No matter how hard I ran, Kenny was always in front. He came in first every time. It bothered me at first before I realized that as long as I kept only him in front of me, everyone else was behind me!

I know what you are thinking. "Well, James, you are just one of those guys who feels coming in second is respectable." Yes. As a 13-year old kid I did feel good about that. This was the first time I felt part of a team. A meaningful member of something that mattered not just to me but to the whole team. We had made it to the finals!

Our final race was about to start. From out team, Kenny and I had made it. As I approached the starting line I looked over my competitors. Most of them stood a full head and shoulders over me.

There I was, just a short, husky kid who could run. The thrill and fear began to surge inside. I felt like I was dangling over a cliff! I backed away from the line and my coach came over, "James, what are you doing?"

"I can't do it coach; I can't."

He looked right at me and replied, "Get back to that line. You can't cop out on me now." Hesitantly I obeyed his direction.

The starter gun went off with a loud bang! The sound startled me and I took off like a scared rabbit! I can remember vividly feeling like I was running for my life. The trail opened up before me, the evergreen trees lined both sides and Kenny was several metres in front of me already.

As we ran, my heart pounded with fear, like the T-Rex was hard on my tail! There was Kenny, quietly striding in front of me. My eyes were glued to him as we ran. After some time, I began to feel more confident as I realized that if he was in front of me, the whole pack was behind me!

The path twisted and turned, Kenny pulled ahead, unaware that I was depending on him. He disappeared from sight and my thoughts wandered back into the fear again! I lost my focus but kept running. Fully amped up, I ran. I ran like I had never before! The trail hit a clearing and turned right. In the clearing a teacher stood as a guide.

I was relieved to see her there, pointing the way. As I neared the clearing a big root crept up to trip me! Like a sack of rocks, I hit the ground face first. All the tension and fear came out in a gush of tears.

The teacher came over, picked me up and dusted me off. I hugged her tightly. Calmly, she hugged me back. For what seemed like several minutes I just let it all out. I heard the footfalls of the pack running by us.

Calmly she looked at me. "You have to finish this James," she said. "You have to finish what you start."

"I can't," I replied. "What will they say about me?"

"It doesn't matter," she said. "Now, finish well James."

Reluctantly I resumed. I ran half-heartedly, knowing I was going to come in last.

It seemed like an eternity running solo through the wooded trail. My thoughts bounced everywhere. Mostly swirling around my fears of what everyone was thinking, how I let the team down. I am sure you can relate.

Rounding the last turn, the woods gave way to an open field. At the finish line stood all the spectators and my team. They enthusiastically cheered me on to the finish line. As I came to a halt, my team gathered around me and were so supportive of my completing the race. Kenny came in first and I was content with that.

What truly surprised me was the team's opposite reaction from what I expected. I expected the worst and they gave me the best. I was not used to this at that time of my life but it changed some of the ways I saw things as a kid. Thank you team!

THE LESSON OF BEING LAST

You might think that this was just a good story. What could be gained from it? We are talking about where in life a mentor or a coach may emerge in the midst of our personal challenges. Let us take a closer look, shall we?

The Peer

I allowed Kenny, my teammate, to set the standard of performance, and he became a Peer in whom I found inspiration to succeed. His results inspired my efforts even though we achieved different results. These achievements were not something I considered threatening. He was humble and competed honestly. I learned how to compete from his example. This is what I would consider positive peer coaching.

Peer coaching is shared through experience and encouragement. It is something found in a team or community where each person finds their own place and is embraced. They are the team that embraces us in our success and in our challenges.

The Team

Similar to peer coaching, the Team (or community) is an essential part of the growing experience. We are social beings by nature and need to feel connected, heard, and embraced.

I have found that change often comes by immersion. In this context; when we spend time with positive people, positive change within us comes about more naturally. The trick is surroung ourselves with positive people.

The Coach

A person who carries authority and our respect will come along to provide appropriate momentum for us when we need it in life. The Coach pushes us to engage those challenges and opportunities. They show us the way to do battle with a healthy respect, fearless engagement, and tireless dedication. The Coach is all about progress and seeks to move us through to the best result.

This is not to say they have no soft side to their influence, but in the times where perseverance is the answer, they do not have that luxury to spend time waiting for us to come around. There are seasons of rest and regrouping, but in the midst of the fight, rest is not what is needed to overcome and win the day.

The Mentor

As the teacher in the clearing patiently waited, so too does the Mentor. It seems Mentors are those who come into view when we are most ready. They are the ones who are focused on the long term and desire to see the best come out from within us. Like the Coach, they will challenge us but in different ways.

In times when we are in that "holding pattern" or rest, their voice can be heard and received. They help us to prepare for the challenges or encourage us to strength again to finish what we start.

I have always felt that Coaches and Mentors are very similar in their goals and influence but as the Mentor pours life, experience, and wisdom into us, the Coach pulls out the potential, progression, and passion from within us.

NEVER GETTING LOST AGAIN

Over the 18 plus years of working with individuals and organized groups, and designing corporate culture, I have learned to uncover and understand problems at the basic foundational roots before working on all the current issues of desire or contention.

It is important to recognize four basic social needs we have as individuals. We all love to be loved, we want to be wanted, we need to be needed, and we want to belong. To find acceptance and appreciation within our community is like a plant finding the sunlight needed to grow. It is the way we are made and one of the ingredients that allows humanity to thrive.

We desire to be a positive contributor to our communities, which requires reconciliations and actions on our part to bring this desire about. We need to figure out what can be done to reconcile with our past so it can empower us to reach our preferred future. Would you agree that it is time to begin taking charge of your direction and ultimate destination? Is it time for a higher quality of life or business?

Has enough time and effort been spent to try to manage or recover things that are now past and beyond your ability to fix? It is time for us to develop a positive attitude of discovery instead of an attitude of constant recovery.

Many of us dwell on things we cannot change and tend to relive those experiences over and over causing adverse affects on our current life perspective. Our negative past binds us and creates a paralytic effect for us in our present circumstances as we relate or compare them to that past. I would ask you to consider the difference between managing life and truly living it.

Before we get into the Compass Philosophy it is vital that we set out some foundational attitudes. In the Everyday coaching style, we believe in the power of choice. Most of our concepts and challenges rely heavily upon the individual's ability to choose and stick to their choices. Choice is the one thing no one can take from us.

Choice

It is your choice to give and to receive. Many of the world's most successful people made a choice to learn and to apply what they learned in practical and relevant circumstances.

When we approach the subject of personal growth and world view, it is crucial to be a humble but pro-active learner. The world does not stop when we decide to lag behind. We are constantly challenged to think differently, think bigger, do better, live larger, move faster, and look deeper. No matter how high the pressure is, at the end of it all you have a choice.

You need to ask yourself three questions:

1. **What do you want?**
2. **What are you willing to do to get there?**
3. **When will you start?**

Firstly, develop some goals. Personal life goals are a foundation to healthy attitudes and pro-active living. Secondly, you need to decide and describe what it is that our life and profession could look like in the near and far future. It may not turn out to be exactly what we see now, but it could be better! At least there is a potential destination to walk toward.

Like a ship on the open water, our lives or business needs a bearing, a map, and a destination. These three aspects produce a sense of purpose, stability, and vital sense of hope in troubled times.

It is now your choice to commit. Ouch!

Commitment feels like a hard task-master, and it can be when life gets rough. However, it is that commitment that fuels the fire to see us through those rough times to a place of victory!

I am now asking you to make these four major commitments:

Commit to Yourself and Own your Success.

It is time to take your personal and professional development to another level. At the end of the day, only you look in the mirror. Be encouraged and decide now how much you want to grow.

Commit to Facing the Challenges.

Do not run, do not dodge, and do not delay. Your time is finite and it only comes around once!

Commit to your Circle.

Accountability is crucial when in development. From whom will you receive encouragement or, dare I say, correction? Over the years, I have learned the value of developing a strong sense of accountability that will carry you through life.

Accountability is the forerunner to establishing integrity. If you cannot learn to be accountable, then how can you expect others to be accountable to you? Many of us go through life looking at the shortcomings of others and believing the other holds the keys to accountability, when in truth, we are usually suffering with the same or worse shortcoming in our own secret lives. A psychologist friend once said to me, "If you can spot it, you most likely got it!" He was half in jest but there is some real truth to this. Think about it.

Commit to Change

In the Everyday Community, we look for people who know the value of change and growth. We hope that our members will actively seek positive change in their lives. Personal elevation is most often achieved by proper and healthy personal excavation.

Keeping Navigation Simple!

Earlier I shared with you how my friend Daniel challenged me with my own set of beliefs and values. The pursuit of Life, Love, Liberty, and Progress was to be my foundational belief for my own navigation. Over time and on demand from clients, we came to develop a simplified philosophy for everyday people and everyday entrepreneurs. The Compass came into being from those four pillars.

THE EVERYDAY COMPASS

NORTH
Navigating your Vibrant Life!

"At one time in human history, people literally depended on their lucky stars for their lives and livelihood. Luckily, they could trust the the Big Dipper and the North Star to guide them. People could sail the seas and cross the trackless deserts without getting lost. When slavery existed in the United States, slaves counted on the Big Dipper (which they called the Drinking Gourd) to show them the North Star."
—*EarthSky.org*

In the northern sky twinkles the North Star. This star is the only star that does not move in the northern hemisphere, which has been a life saver to many travelers and sailors from becoming hopelessly lost. No matter where they were, if they could find their bearings with that star, they could find their way home again.

Like that north star, what we believe in should become a stable set of principles that we can always draw back to when we find ourselves troubled or when those hard decisions come. It doesn't mean that those beliefs and principles never change, but they should remain constant and reliable as our life moves forward.

This metaphor describes our personal set of beliefs and values that act as a constant point of reference to guide us to our preferred destination. What does it mean to believe?

To Believe:
To have confidence in the truth, the existence, or the reliability of something, although without absolute proof that one is right in doing so. Only if one believes in something can one act purposefully.

Personal Value:
To consider with respect to worth, excellence, usefulness, or importance.

Personal Principle:
A guiding sense of the requirements and obligations of right conduct: a person of principle.

The first two definitions are regarded as actions and not stagnant concepts that only require a mental acknowledgement. To believe in a certain way of behaving, to have certain values for treating others or standards of performance, is key to making progress through any life challenge.

These beliefs also serve as foundational standards for decision-making both in a tactical sense and in a moral sense. These guiding beliefs or principles form an internal framework that help protect us from deception, manipulation, and confusion.

For example, if you believe that "treating others the way you would like to be treated" is your personal value principle for living, then that positive principle guides your personal choices, attitudes, and actions toward others in many types of circumstances. It is the way you do things and you may carry a hope that others will reciprocate in kind. This belief would likely create good will with others.

If you believe that "the pursuit of personal excellence" is important, then that value would assist you in making choices regarding that standard. Hopefully it would propel you to higher goal achievement and better practices when working with others. It is an inspiring value of motivation. It simply is just the way you do it.

North is: "What we believe" and "Why we do it this way."

A Belief that Builds Influence!

"Every soldier must know, before he goes into battle, how the little battle he is to fight fits into the larger picture, and how the success of his fighting will influence the battle as a whole."

—Bernard Law Montgomery

I have not yet met anyone who has not desired to do something good in the world. Building influence is like a chemical chain reaction. One thing must be established before another thing can become reality which leads to a larger result.

Let us explore the chain reaction of building positive influence:

Belief > Principles & Values > Ethics > Choice > Actions

What Blocked My Way?

Years ago as I sat reading one of my favourite authors, Derek Prince, I discovered this truth about people and how they influence others in their surrounding environment. He stated "If you know the root, you will understand the fruit." On the surface, that sounds like no great revelation, but what it implies is truly profound when trying to understand and help people.

The principle is that if you understand the beginning, the depth of the past, and the marks they leave on our souls, you can extrapolate why we have a certain behavior in the present day. For example, in most cases, divorce between a married couple does not happen overnight. Usually, years of bad habits, misunderstandings, unresolved issues, or unmet expectations compound to negative effect. Divorce happens when one person or both have reached "the final straw". That final conflict erupts and the couple calls it quits.

The root of the example is not the divorce (the "fruit" of the relationship), but rather the unresolved hurt — unanswered and unaccounted for so long. Finally, one day, something is said, something was or was not done, and the bubble bursts.

I Cannot Give What I Do Not Have

One season of my own life, unresolved conflicts and hurts had piled up from certain people with whom I worked through my college years. They affected everything I put my hands to and I became so focused on the problem that there was little room for new people and experiences in my life. I needed to do something radical.

I know what you might be thinking: the problem was with me; I carried the issue and not them. You would be right, to a point.

Sure, personalities conflict, but the resulting insult that occurred was devastating to me so early in my professional development. After 5 years of carrying these offenses in my heart I had to do something to alleviate the pain and eliminate the emotional obstacle in front of me. I was silently angry and disappointed. It showed mostly in my family life and through my frustrating discontentment in my professional life.

Late one night, my family had gone to bed. That lonely desk light, the quiet… the moment of truth can in a moment of deep reflection. I finally decided that my family and personal happiness was worth way more than my anger, fear, and pride. Coming face-to-face with the man in the mirror, I realized I woul not be able to lead others to freedom until I had first endured the journey myself!

Finding the Will to Act

After some thought and a little prayer, I resolved to write letters to each person outlining what I felt the problem was. I included a vital extension of forgiveness so that I could find freedom from the hurt. But that was not all. I felt there needed to be a measure of weight carried on my shoulders for my part. So, in the letter, I also asked for their forgiveness for my past attitudes and that when we met again, we could hopefully start over in a new context and on level ground.

After I delivered each letter, I was relieved that I could feel clear in conscience and from those dark clouds of condemnation that lingered in my mind. This process was more about setting me free and less about the justice I might have felt by just stating my case. I was not as concerned about what they would think, so long as I obeyed my conscience on the matter. The greater result was that I could take responsibility to clear my own mind and soul of the matter and achieve a sense of freedom from that season of life.

I present this concept to you so that you may feel empowered to do something about those lingering hurts that do nothing but cloud your mind and stop you from finding direction.

This is to help bring clarity as well as to make room for new relationships!

The "Chemical Catalyst"

Catalyst is defined as "a substance that increases the rate of a chemical reaction without itself undergoing any permanent chemical change."

Belief changes EVERYTHING! Just believe! (Find your North Star.)

Before we can fully understand our present reactions and conduct in the face of current situations, it is important to recognize what we specifically believe about these circumstances. These beliefs form the basis of our personal reactions, influence our choices which positively or negatively affect others around us.

There are two ways to present this topic of personal beliefs:

1.   We can look at it as having a set of beliefs per our worldview and spiritual faith practice.

2.   We can focus on our beliefs that have been formed through personal experience.

Either way, having a system of personal belief works to help us cope in the world within which we live. Let us take this time to focus upon the latter.

Beliefs Formed Through Experience

Our influence can be positive or negative depending on how we have received our experiences in the past. For example, if a child experienced a consistent negative influence from their teachers growing up, he or she might tend to believe that people in the teaching profession do not care and are indifferent to their own personal wellbeing.

Of course, this is a generalization: many great teachers are faithfully doing excellent work. But in this illustration, because the child has only what he or she experienced, the basis of his or her belief about teachers would most likely be based primarily on those past experiences. Until someone plays an instrumental role in providing a positive correction, the child may hold onto that belief which would likely manifest itself through a deep mistrust for authority figures in later life.

By this example, I am attempting to provide a basis of common understanding that what has been experienced can cause a set of beliefs to be established. These beliefs would create a reaction whether positive or negative or even just a more cautious reaction to similar influences and circumstances in the future.

For this reason, it would be considered vital to recalibrate current beliefs when pursuing personal growth. Once this is set in motion, a person can then establish a new vision for what they choose to believe about their life, personal values, and the world around them. From this foundation will arise a new and hopefully positive perspective.

To Value (or *having personal values*):
To regard or esteem highly.

To have personal values is to understand the word "value" as a verb or an action. As a person believing in certain things, we will form a set of values (beliefs or convictions that manifest through active principles of character and conduct) from which we will pull daily. For example, I believe that having love for others is vital. Therefore, my values might say, "community is a key element for healthy living" which simply means I value the influence of positive people in my life.

Ethics:
That branch of philosophy dealing with values relating to human conduct, with respect to the rightness and wrongness of certain actions and to the goodness and badness of the motives and ends of such actions."

A system of moral principles: the ethics of a culture.

Ethics are the framework of moral actions and conduct within any social arena. These are the internal rules that help us determine certain outcomes through our decision making. I believe ethics are personal structures that have been formed from our beliefs and values over the span of our lives.

For example, if I believe that love for others is vital, my values will state that I value the positive influence of others in my life. My ethics built upon those two foundations would assist me in making a right decision when asked if I would harm another person or not within a given circumstance. If the situation violated my beliefs and values, my ethics tell me that it would be wrong for me to harm another person.

An argument can be made that in survival situations ethics might take a back seat, but a counter argument can be made that we hold principles to justify the avoidance of discomfort caused by ethical tensions and conduct.

What I am hoping to communicating here is that ethics is a healthy and higher form of social and personal maturity. They display self-control and build personal credibility. Consistent ethical behavior assists in building trust in the minds and hearts of those around us. Would you like to feel trusted?

Choice:
The act of choosing.

It is as simple as that. Choice is the act of choosing. But how we choose is dictated by a multitude of factors at any given moment. These factors range from primal survival and self-preservation to an elaborate balance of cause and effect usually deemed to be within our favour.

I believe a choice is the final product found within our beliefs, values for living, and ethics for conduct. What we choose when faced with certain social dilemmas or physical circumstances can make or break our ability to attract, influence, and maintain quality relationships.

Influence:
The effect one person has upon another.

It is very much like a good or bad aroma. Over the years I have found that people in general are intuitive and more often feel if we are a good fit for relationship or not. If our internal character qualities are less than desirable it can be felt through our personal countenance, body language and overall attitude toward our environment. The result of our influence is deemed healthy by engaging conversation or deemed unhealthy by a typical silent resignation and withdrawal from others we meet.

Action:
Actions, habitual or usual acts; conduct.

They say "Actions speak louder than words." I agree. In context of the chain reaction, our actions are the obvious "fruit" of our inner "roots". What we do will be the most visible display of what we are. We can shout out our most cherished beliefs but if we lack the conviction to follow them, people will quickly determine our quality and whether they will stay within our influence or not.

It takes courage to make the right choices in life and even more courage to live by them. One of the major questions from leaders addresses that silent expectation that people have regarding their consistency. Do we do what we say we will do? Will we remain consistent in our actions so that people find it easier to trust in us?

The consistency and harmony of our actions is what people will tend to build their trust on in a relationship. People can forgive mistakes or even the learning curves life seems to throw at us, but when they discover a deliberate betrayal of conduct in comparison to what we said we believed or valued, it is over.

Ask yourself, "If I need people to have integrity, am I a person of integrity?" or "If I am obsessive about certain things in a relationship, are my expectations unreasonable or am I hypocritical in those expectations?"

Maybe go so far as to ask "If it were me, could I live up to those expectations that I have imposed on others?"

Result:

To spring, arise, or proceed as a consequence of actions, circumstances, premises, etc.; be the outcome.

Our results are the testimony of our quality as people. These are the things that speak of our story and memory long after we are gone from this earth. My hope is that our friends and clients would value the end results and live with no regret because of the positive "ripple effect" they have caused during their time.

This concept is an unselfish way of living and is not easy to attain. However, I believe it is worth every pain, every point of perseverance that we experience. I don't believe most of us truly wants to live a life carrying the weight of a negative influence, the weight of a bad result caused by our choices and actions.

To conclude, the chain reaction starts deep within us. It is time to have the courage to look within and decide if your current results with people are what you envision and desire.

If not, then it may be time to go on a journey of personal discovery!

EAST
Who We Spend Our Precious Time With!

The direction of East represents our community. Who we decide to surround ourselves with is a vital aspect to a healthy life experience. I have always said, "If we desire to be a leader, hang out with leaders. If we want to be positive, hang out with positive people." This is a core value for building our Everyday Community.

Community is important for all kinds of reasons. A positive community can provide influence for good choices, great ideas for problem solving, shared experiences, as well as helpful resources for when we are in need. Who do you spend time with? It takes wisdom to know who we allow to influence our life and of whom we may need to steer clear.

> *"By wisdom a house is built, and through understanding it is established; through knowledge its rooms are filled with rare and beautiful treasures,"*
>
> —*King Solomon*

I have had the privilege of learning much from others in life. I saw these experiences as a given opportunity to observe the actions — good or bad — of others closest to me. It boils down to this: I could gain good knowledge or avoid calamity if my eyes and ears were open.

Paying attention to the fast-moving world around us is essential to a positive personal growth experience. I have met many who desire to grow in their life but decline the opportunities to take risks, meet new people, and experience new life.

Three big lessons that I have learned and passed on to my own sons. Can I take a few moments and share them with you?

The First Lesson

When it comes to relating to people and building our understanding about them, we can at least learn how to be, or how NOT to be. I have found that by listening, observing, and helping others, the biggest lessons can be caught without any direct teaching whatsoever.

People will teach you through their attitudes, choices and experiences; how to govern yourself accordingly in the future. So, if you can't learn anything specific from someone, you can at least learn one of these aspects.

The Second Lesson

"A smart man learns from his own mistakes; a wise man learns from the mistakes of others!" Better to take lessons from others in their journey (and thus empower our ability to make right and healthy choices for living), than to continually charge straight into a painful experience with our heads down. This way of learning costs too much and wastes valuable time! I will not deny that we may have to learn through our own experiences, but if unnecessary pain can be avoided, why not avoid it?

The Third Lesson

The definition of wisdom is *knowledge applied rightly*. Wisdom is experience that we have learned from and can apply its value and teaching in future circumstances.

Wisdom in life empowers us to make the right choice. This wonderful concept enables us to shake free from negative feelings of our past and begin to provide a positive influence to others in the present. We are tremendously empowered to be influential!

East is: The community we walk with and that supports us in our endeavours. They gladly accept and challenge us because they care about us.

Social Immersion

I truly understand why some people are hesitant to engage groups of people or have become fearful in social settings. Some of those reasons may be justified in the short term, but they should not keep us from experiencing the joy of laughter and authentic fellowship with others.

Phobia:

A persistent, irrational fear of a specific object, activity, or situation that leads to a compelling desire to avoid it.

This concept is generally interpreted as a fear of death by the object/activity/situation you are trying to avoid.

Sounds extreme, does it not? Perhaps your first reaction to this definition was, "Well, that is certainly NOT me!" Yet because of prior experiences, you might carry feelings of wariness around people. Some of us may have a phobia of social situations.

"Social immersion" is like stepping into a hot tub. Have you ever leaped into a hot tub?

Hopefully not, simply because of the extreme change in temperature. We tend to take our time, slowly sinking ourselves deeper as our body adapts to the new temperature.

Why can't the process of building social confidence be like that?

With that being said, I present to you the concept of **Social Immersion:**

An action taken to address and minimize the debilitating feelings that prevent us from forming new and vibrant relationships.

This action is a risk that can produce an astounding result for you and those with whom you engage!

The action I suggest here is to take initiative and get involved with a community that represents a cause or purpose that means something to you. I don't mean taking on a membership that you never attend. I mean really get involved where there is a great reason for coming together and producing something as a community. Your part could be small but no less meaningful.

This action must take you beyond a mental ascent to a multi-faceted interaction whereby you become positively affected and begin to produce a ripple effect of life-giving influence!

The risk of not taking action is to simply continue doing what you have been doing and hope something changes. Almost sounds like the definition of insanity does it not?

SOUTH
Achieving Personal Liberty!

I like to think of South as the direction of the past. It is the accumulation of experiences from which we have learned, that help us to make better choices, make better relationships, and draw from valuable lessons learned.

I encourage many to take the time to consider this direction carefully to find room for reconciliation and forgiveness, to clear our mind and heart in preparation for greater adventures!

Life Lessons
The Buried Treasure of Our Past

Taking a healthy personal inventory of our life experience produces personal growth! The gaining of wisdom is a vital quest with a precious outcome.

> *"For wisdom will enter your heart, and knowledge will be pleasant to your soul. Discretion will protect you, and understanding will guard you."*

—*King Solomon*

Let us agree that active learning from our past and from the experiences of others is of great benefit. As the youngest of five brothers there was ample opportunity to learn from the choices of my older siblings! That doesn't mean I avoided all of their hard choices, but it does mean that as the youngest I had been given the opportunity to observe the actions good or bad of others closest to me.

The bottom line is that I could gain good knowledge or avoid calamity if my eyes, ears, mind, and heart were open to learning from my experiences and from those around me.

Carpe Diem!

When life gives you an opportunity for reconciliation or closure, take it! This was made very clear during a speaking engagement I conducted in my early twenties.

Around 1989 I received an invitation to speak at a men's group event. The topic was focused on what it meant to give a young man a chance to excel. It was a great event; the attendees were happy and welcoming. I felt a sense of satisfaction and the joy of a job well done. After the ninety-minute meeting we reconvened at the local restaurant for breakfast.

As we sat talking, I looked around and discovered someone sitting at the other side of the restaurant, sharing breakfast casually with a woman. It was my grade six teacher, Mr. Turner. My first reaction: I quietly froze inside.

What is the story with Mr. Turner, you are asking? Well, my school experiences were not very warm and fuzzy to say the least. During my grade six year, Mr. Turner and I had several "differences of opinion" to put it mildly. We suffered from angry-kid/intolerant-teacher syndrome.

I don't recall all our specifics but what I can tell you is that it was an oppressive experience to be in his class. He was a classic adult-bully if he did not like you. For my part I am sure I gave him ample ammunition! It got to such a point that I had been frequently removed from class even for the slightest offence. Assess this however you wish but what I remember most is the rejection and harshness of how I had been treated.

I do appreciate the value of developing the right skills to deal with conflict and adversity. In fact, I highly support the lesson of having a tough skin. What I don't support is the unnecessary treatment that kids do receive from adults in authority who will not, or cannot rise above their feelings when working with children. These bad memories stuck with me for a long time. This was just one of many "thorns in the flesh" I carried as a young man.

Looking across the floor, I felt an internal pull to act. What I needed to act on I wasn't sure. Before I knew it, I was walking toward Mr. Turner's table. In those brief moments of thought, I realized I had three choices: One, I could walk back and do nothing and thus continue carrying my offence. Two, I could walk over and let him have it. I could finally have my say and get it off my chest. Or three, I could calmly forgive him and be released.

I arrived at his table, he looked up at me and I looked right at him. I made the choice. With a slight tremble, I proceeded to ask, "Mr. Turner?"

"Yes?" he replied.

"My name is James Burgess; I was in your grade six class at College Street Public School in 1980." He sat silent. "I was the kid you put in the hallway almost every day."

Holding myself steady inside, what I said next was like getting a 10-tonne weight off my shoulders.

"I want to tell you that I am about to enter into seminary to become a minister. I know this may not mean much to you, but I just wanted you to know that." Then, without another word, I walked back to my table feeling numb from the experience of facing this issue down.

The true value of this chance meeting did not hit me fully until later in life. What happened here was a full reconciliation of my past whereby I could find closure to something I had carried for years, and unlike when I wrote the letters, I was able to take advantage of the moment because I was paying attention it. After this, the hurtful rejection I carried from that time had melted away because I gathered the courage to let it go. Since then, I have been able to confidently empower many others to freedom. For that, I thank God.

The Value of Paying Attention!

Paying attention to the fast-moving world around us is essential to a growing as a person. I have met many who desire to grow in their life but decline the opportunities to take risks. They only want to meet new people and experience new life in the safe and familiar. This circumspect attitude may feel right in the moment, but only serves to further limit our courage and progress toward our preferred future.

When we pay attention, we not only learn from our experiences but also can apply everyone else's lessons. These are the stories that we pass on to the next generation.

I cannot stress enough how valuable it is for us to take a close look at our experiences and decide how to best utilize them to provide wisdom to others. Discovering the value of our life-lessons whether good, bad, or ugly is truly evidence of maturity. I encourage you to find closure, learn from it all, not just from those safe/familiar experiences or from the things that are comfortable for you to embrace. The challenge is to achieve perspective beyond yourself and provide a better influence to the world around you.

South is: Our reconciled past. What we have learned and how to apply those valuable lessons to empower our future.

WEST
Uncompromising Progress!

West has been thought of as the direction of exploration and pioneering. It is deep within the North American cultures to explore, innovate, and create new ways of solving problems. We need to take risks and explore life.

One survey by paperpulpit.com was taken years ago of senior citizens, and one astounding sentiment came forward. They overwhelmingly said that if they could do it over again, they would take more risks.

Getting Beyond the Breakers

"Breaking Out!"

In every life, our choices will have sacrifices tied to them. Working through a painful past requires a focused and uncompromising commitment to breaking free from its paralyzing effects. Is this something that you are working through? Are you having trouble finding that elusive place of personal peace over your past?

Years ago, my wife and I came to some very discomforting conclusions regarding our community and associations. We realized that things needed to change in our lives. I felt at the time like I was drinking polluted water. It was a slow-damage-over-time way of living.

Where we spent our time and efforts had given us a false sense of purpose and value, but we lacked mutual benefit to our family. Like the polluted water, that lack was not enough to cause a drastic pain, but over time the polite indifference we received eroded our confidence from the inside. We could not escape the feeling that there was more for us in this life. Sound familiar?

My purpose for sharing this is to awaken greater senses of purpose, destination, and value (for time and personal satisfaction).

However, please note that these kinds of personal growth benefits do not come without cost.

Our choices tested our resolve regarding our vision for the future that my wife and I carried within us. The reactions from people we thought were long-time friends showed us a harsh truth about the nature of many in the world. I may sound cynical, but I really want to stress that this painful realization will bring you freedom.

It was painful at the onset of this experience, but I can't adequately express to you the incredible release we have achieved by enduring this time of personal discomfort. It was like a season of social surgery.

We don't wish this pain on others, but the process is certainly valuable for its outcome. We are now free from the pressure of living with aimless connections.

I can say that within a year of making this vital life-direction change, I was actively pursuing four of my six established life goals that I had recorded earlier in my life. It was like the release of a tightly coiled spring! I became a happier and more satisfied person as a result of taking positive action in spite of the existing challenges and circumstances around that time of life.

I am not saying that to break out is all about departing from a community. It is more about recognizing the need to break out from a negative situation to pursue a positive situation. My example is a story I would later find to be of great value when building the Everyday Community and its culture of "success found together"!

"Breaking Through!"

When we think of the term "breakthrough", it usually conjures up images like a sprinter breaking the finish line with excessive strain. Maybe you see something different, like friends toasting your latest achievement. Both pictures are accurate when considering the end result. But is there more to this story?

Let us examine that champion sprinter. Take a moment to visualize the hours upon hours of training. All those early-morning runs, those gruelling sessions in the presence of a demanding coach.

Think of all the temptations felt when watching friends enjoy that sumptuous piece of cheesecake while maintaining determination to continue with the raw veggies. Funny, but true!

Imagine now all the emotional jitters felt and confidence-building pep talks needed along the way. How about all the races leading up to this one shining moment of breakthrough? What about the losses? The internal process of emotional recovery, finding new courage to continue training. What about continually having to gather up that strength to race again, and again developing and galvanizing that resolve to do better each time. Got the picture?

All that being said, now consider the one ingredient needed to break through. This one ingredient for personal growth is often hard to coach with many demands on our attitude and personal resources. It will tax every part of us while reminding us of the prized outcome we are focusing on. All of the testing and the pain of change is worth it. It is an ingredient that fulfills every part of a breakthrough life experience. That ingredient is perseverance.

Perseverance:
Steadfastness in doing something despite difficulty or delay in achieving success.

My encouragement for you is simple. An old proverb says, "If you have perseverance, you lack nothing."

If you have taken the time to see your life from a bigger point of view and have established those life goals mentioned earlier, then perseverance is the final ingredient needed from which to act appropriately.

I dare you to ask out loud: "Why does having perseverance mean we lack nothing?" Be prepared for the adventure that will come. Enjoy the ride!

"Breaking Forth!"

I have taught my children since they were little that part of my job as a caring parent is to build them launch pads from which they can use to achieve success in any area. I never promised that I was going to do it all for them. There has to be a point where they discover the thrill of flight for themselves. This philosophy has never hurt them, only empowered them.

Breaking forth sounds like an explosive and violent emergence of new energy and potential. At some point a move needs to be made to produce a preferred result or a materialization of a greater quality of life and achievement.

In my travels I see so many who have a very limited view of the world, they walk ignorantly through life not even noticing beauty or excitement around them and never exploring their own potential.

Maybe they walk like this because they were never properly informed, not educated on the concept of exploration and possibility. Is it because the world needs certain people to be simple "worker ants"? I don't know about you, but it gets me steamed to think that mediocrity is an acceptable standard of life experience for many who, if given the opportunity (or launch pad), might actually excel!

It is incumbent on all of us to take initiative and search out new possibilities and positive changes. No one can do this for us. But we need to lay the right foundations for people and to provide an opening whereby a choice can be made. At least if they choose, they have a greater chance to own their chosen outcomes. Right?

What does "breaking forth" mean to you? If given the right set of circumstances, what would you endeavour to achieve? What influence would you provide to assist the world in making positive change? We all have a part!

I realized long ago that I — as one man — could not save the world, but — as one man — I could influence the world within my reach. Then I began to own that truth. Things began to happen at that crossroads of understanding. Now is your time. The fact that you are even engaging in personal growth is evidence that you have it in you to succeed and achieve greater influence. What action will you take now that you have this choice?

The Choice Is Yours!

Choose to reconcile the past!
(Find closure)

Choose to stand out!
(Break from mediocrity)

Choose to break from mediocrity!
(Create an impact)

Choose to change and persevere!
(Grow and explore)

Choose to love this life worth living!
(Share your best with others)

Choose to be a catalyst for goodwill!
(Improve your environment wherever you go)

A healthy risk now and then is good. A healthy risk does not mean a thoughtless risk (nor does it always mean an extreme sport activity). These risks are explorative moves which could be as simple as trying a new food. Perhaps try a new hobby, sport, or meet new people.

Maybe start a new business and explore the dynamics of building value and financially achieving goals. Whatever it may look like, this is the start of a new thing!

**West is: Where we are going and what will we discover!
Having an attitude of discovery and not one of continual
recovery!**

KNOW YOUR COMPASS!

When I was in grade school, we learned about orienteering and how to read maps and navigate the wilderness. It was interesting to me at the time and I enjoyed the idea of plotting a course or path to a chosen destination.

My classmates and I were challenged to locate certain points of interest in the area using a map and compass as well as a little team work. It was fun because, though we could see topographical information on the map, it did not show us visually what the terrain actually looked like. So, the fun was seeing the destination on the map, then discovering it in full colour when we arrived.

What I have learned is that the compass does not reveal the terrain that is traveled in detail. Sometimes we travel toward something and we do not have sight of, nor control over, the terrain between where we currently are and where it is we want to get to. The compass is a tool that we use to keep our sense of direction and confidence when we are not capable of "seeing the forest for the trees" so to speak.

For myself, I enjoy the adventure of the sea. If you are in a position of leadership or business, you will appreciate the concept of the captain and crew. The captain plots the course and the crew fulfill their duties to sail the ship toward its goal. Like finding a buried treasure or discovering a new world, your life and business embark upon a journey to claim the best bounty.

THE EVERYDAY COMPASS
We Are Pathfinders!

Everyday Foundational Coaching Philosophy

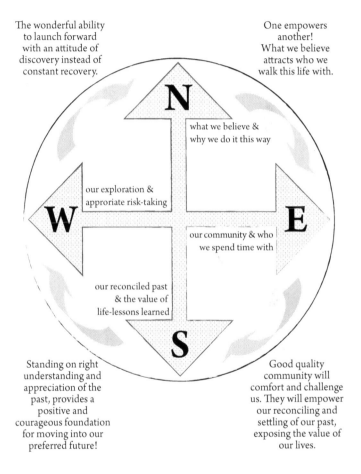

The wonderful ability to launch forward with an attitude of discovery instead of constant recovery.

One empowers another! What we believe attracts who we walk this life with.

N

what we believe & why we do it this way

our exploration & approriate risk-taking

W

E

our community & who we spend time with

our reconciled past & the value of life-lessons learned

S

Standing on right understanding and appreciation of the past, provides a positive and courageous foundation for moving into our preferred future!

Good quality community will comfort and challenge us. They will empower our reconciling and settling of our past, exposing the value of our lives.

FREEDOM WITH CONSCIENCE

Many years ago, I sat listening as hard as I could to one of my most respected professors and the college president. The student body was assemble to launch a new school year and there was a wild anticipation in the air for our future conquests.

This defining moment took me more than 12 years to apply to my life and business with any real clarity and strength. I recognized that my life was bigger than the singular moment of now — that in fact, it was an eternal cycle of value and influence that I could create. We are given only one life and I did not want mine to go by with nothing to show for it.

As the professor shouted "Good News!" my spirit shivered. I will never forget his three primary values: live with nothing to prove, live with nothing to hide, live with nothing to lose. These were not the thoughtless and reckless notions of youthful abandonment. They were given as vital principles for living a life of freedom with conscience. It was one of the best mentoring moments of my life!

These three values are by no means easy to accomplish. It takes a lifetime to work on our personal character. The good news is that that work is progress toward perfection! Making the right choice when working with others is a reward in and of itself. I am not always successful in living up to it, but by grace, I can certainly look to my "North" and choose to feel empowered to conduct myself accordingly!

Living with Nothing to Prove

Living with nothing to prove is not to say that we arrogantly "flip the bird" to everyone else. Nor is it a stubborn attitude that denies common sense or positive influence. It has more to do with getting to points of personal satisfaction and becoming settled in our own skin.

The battle against personal insecurity is tough, but with healthy self-examination from time-to- time, we might have a chance to stand with confidence instead of pushing back with that unnecessary and annoying self-defence.

"The unexamined life is not worth living."

—*Socrates*

Living with Nothing to Hide

Transparency is tough too! We all hide things inside. I am not attempting to tackle the issues of deep personal secrets here — I would rather leave that to your personal coach or therapist!

What does need to be highlighted here is the value of a clear conscience. I have always told my sons that when I make decisions in my business, one marker of whether it is the right decision is how it affects my quality of sleep. Yes, you read it correctly!

It is simple: if I sleep soundly, I feel I have a clear conscience about my current decisions and circumstances. Being confident in my decisions settles me down and reduces anxiousness.

Self-accountability is a vital part of personal growth and an important aspect of leadership, influence, personal achievement, and credibility. If we cannot master this aspect of life, why do we think we can hold others to a standard that we will not hold ourselves to? What do we become? Untrustworthy hypocrites. I enjoy being trusted; how about you?

Living with Nothing to Lose

This one is easy to misinterpret. At first glance you might think that I am teaching people to live in reckless abandonment. Nope.

To live free is to live life with integrity and responsibility.

The concept of having nothing to lose is to "hang on to it all loosely". When working with families in debt recovery, I often find our discussions focusing on the pain and strain of making a new life with new standards. I try to encourage that while they are in a time of "financial recalibration", things or money can be replaced. Time cannot.

Sometimes we need to release things, hang-ups, and offences and walk with the understanding of a gardener. We need personal pruning from time-to-time in order to be prepared for greater things.

Since that day long ago, I have held these values close to my heart knowing that they will be part of a compass that will define my dealings with people. Through all of this time, I have come to understand my own personal mandate for living. It is the mandate of encouragement.

This mandate is to spark a positive energetic stimulation for living well, to cultivate empathy and community, and to activate action from apathy in the lives of others.

What Mandate Do You Carry?

These values form a core set of beliefs I carry that allow me to experience change and growth even during our times of hardship. Like the old British army saying goes, "Pain is weakness escaping!"

I believe I am a better man because of it. That may sound weird, but things that are beyond explanation often are. Like the quote earlier in the book, we can have the freedom of the whole ocean because we have become a servant to the compass. Are you ready for this grand adventure? It is time to sail beyond your breakers!

THANK YOU

Enjoy this life, friend. Plot your course; record your findings; share it with others every day.

Sincerely,

James P. Burgess Lead Coach

Everyday Communities Inc.

ABOUT THE AUTHOR

James Burgess is the founder of the Everyday Communities and the main creator of the Everyday community coaching methodology.

He has authored 3 major coaching courses: Insight Sales & Small Business Development, Take Flight Personal Coaching Course, and the S.E.E. Program for debt restructuring (in collaboration with Parley Debt Consulting); as well as being an active content creator for coaching and mentoring online.

As a practical and innovative coach, James works with many small-business entrepreneurs to provide successful business development tactics and strategies that are proven to provide success even in tough economic times.

James and the Everyday Communities also provide effective personal development coaching for families and individuals seeking to find their passion, purpose, and personal empowerment.

James has spoken to a variety of corporate teams and communities and has performed memorable facilitation through customized retreats and training workshops.

For almost 20 years, James and his wife Sharon have been working passionately to assist their clients and community in finding their success through their Everyday Compass coaching philosophy.

52632608R00042

Made in the USA
San Bernardino, CA
25 August 2017